Motocross Cycles

BY JACK DAVID

TORQUE™

BELLWETHER MEDIA • MINNEAPOLIS, MN

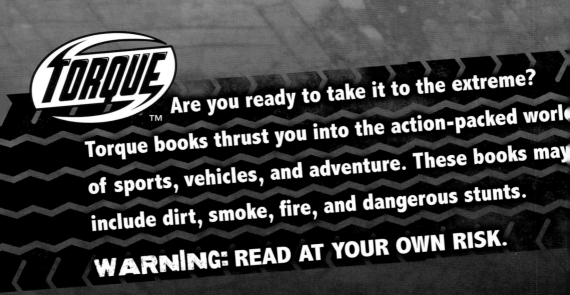

Are you ready to take it to the extreme? Torque books thrust you into the action-packed world of sports, vehicles, and adventure. These books may include dirt, smoke, fire, and dangerous stunts.

WARNING: READ AT YOUR OWN RISK.

This edition first published in 2008 by Bellwether Media.

No part of this publication may be reproduced in whole or in part without written permission of the publisher. For information regarding permission, write to Bellwether Media Inc., Attention: Permissions Department, Post Office Box 19349, Minneapolis, MN 55419.
Library of Congress Cataloging-in-Publication Data

David, Jack, 1968-
  Motocross cycles / by Jack David.
    p. cm. -- (Torque--cool rides)
  Summary: "Full color photography accompanies engaging information about Motocross Cycles. The combination of high-interest subject matter and light text is intended for students in grades 3 through 7"--Provided by publisher.
  Includes bibliographical references and index.
  ISBN-13: 978-1-60014-152-2 (hardcover : alk. paper)
  ISBN-10: 1-60014-152-8 (hardcover : alk. paper)
  1. Trail bikes--Juvenile literature. 2. Motorcycles, Racing--Juvenile literature. 3. Motocross--Juvenile literature. I. Title.

  TL441.D372 2008
  629.227'5--dc22

                                                2007040566

Contents

What Is a Motocross Cycle?

Motocross cycles are made for all kinds of action. They sail through the air. They kick up dirt. They bump, skid, and speed to the finish line.

Motocross cycles are dirt bikes designed for racing. They're light, fast, and easy to handle on rough surfaces. Riders race them on twisting motocross and **supercross** courses. They launch them off high dirt jumps. Some riders even do risky stunts in the air.

MotoCross Cycle History

Motorcycle racing has been popular for close to 100 years. Dirt racing started in England in the 1920s. Riders rode their cross-country motorcycles in races called **scrambles**.

9

The high-flying sport of motocross grew out of these scrambles. It started in Europe and later came to the United States. Motocross and supercross races were drawing thousands of fans by the 1980s. **Motocross freestyle** emerged in the 1990s. Fans love to watch riders do jaw-dropping stunts on their motocross cycles.

Fast FaCt

Most motocross cycles are built by the "Big Four" Japanese manufacturers: Honda, Kawasaki, Suzuki, and Yamaha.

Parts of a MotoCross Cycle

Motocross cycles are lightweight, powerful, and tough. The metal frame is called the **chassis**. The chassis is usually made of **aluminum**. Aluminum is extremely strong and lightweight. The body panels fit over the chassis.

A motocross cycle needs a strong
suspension system. This system connects
the chassis to the wheels. Springs and shock
absorbers help give the bike a smooth ride
over rough surfaces.

Bikes must be able to withstand the big jumps and hard landings of the sport. Dirt and mud courses don't offer much **traction**. Motocross cycles need "knobby" tires with deep **tread**. The bumps and grooves of the tread give the tires a good grip.

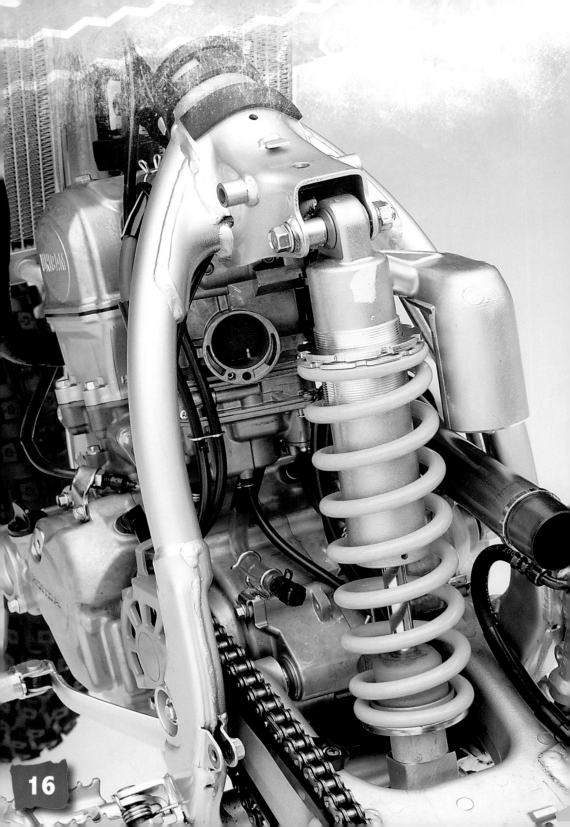

Motocross cycles are classed by engine size. Engines are measured in cubic centimeters (cc). Common classes include 125cc, 250cc, and the super-powerful 500cc.

17

Motocross Cycles in Action

Motocross and supercross races are thrilling events. About 20 riders start each race. They often bump and crash into each other as they fight for position. The bikes sail over huge jumps and skid around sharp turns. Motocross courses are outdoors. Most are about 2 miles (3.2 kilometers) long. Supercross courses are located in indoor stadiums. Organizers haul in mountains of dirt to make the roughest, most exciting course possible.

Fast FaCt

In motocross freestyle, a "superman" is stretching your body above the bike with your hands on the handlebars.

Motocross freestyle is a wild sport. Riders speed up huge dirt jumps. They fly into the air and do dangerous tricks. Some riders do backflips. Others swing their legs up over the handlebars or hold on with only their hands. The fans roar as they watch the skilled riders handle their machines.

Glossary

aluminum—a strong, lightweight metal

chassis—the metal frame of a motocross cycle

motocross freestyle—a motocross sport in which riders perform tricks off a huge dirt jump

scrambles—the name given to the earliest dirt bike races in England in the 1920s

supercross—a sport in which riders race motorcycles on dirt courses built in indoor stadiums

suspension system—a set of springs and shock absorbers that connect the chassis of a motocross cycle to its wheels

traction—the grip of the tires on a riding surface

tread—the series of bumps and grooves on a tire that help it grip rough surfaces

To Learn More

AT THE LIBRARY

David, Jack. *Moto-X Freestyle*. Minneapolis, Minn.: Bellwether, 2008.

David, Jack. *Motocross Racing*. Minneapolis, Minn.: Bellwether, 2008.

Levy, Janey. *Motocross Races*. New York: PowerKids Press, 2007.

ON THE WEB

Learning more about motocross cycles is as easy as 1, 2, 3.

1. Go to www.factsurfer.com

2. Enter "motocross cycles" into search box.

3. Click the "Surf" button and you will see a list of related web sites.

With factsurfer.com, finding more information is just a click away.

Index

The images in this book are reproduced through the courtesy of: Keith Robinson, front cover; American Honda Motor Co., Inc., pp. 4-5, 12-13, 16, 17; Yamaha Motor Corporation, pp. 6, 11; Aris Messinis/Getty Images, p. 7; Topical Press Agency/ Stringer/Getty Images, p. 9; J. Edmunds/Shazamm/ESPN Images, p. 10; Pete Demos/Shazamm/ESPN Images, pp. 14-15; R. Archer/KTM Sportmotorcycle AG, p. 18; Bakke/Shazamm/ESPN Images, pp. 20-21.